Ultimate Bill *and* Mail Organizer

for Busy Professionals

@ Journals and Notebooks

All Rights reserved. No part of this book may be reproduced or used in any way or form or by any means whether electronic or mechanical, this means that you cannot record or photocopy any material ideas or tips that are provided in this book.

Copyright 2016

Bill Log _____ Month

✓	Date Paid	Bill Name	Amount	Due Date	Confirmation

Mail Tracker

Date	Sender	Date	Sender

Bill Log _____ Month

✓	Date Paid	Bill Name	Amount	Due Date	Confirmation

Mail Tracker

Date	Sender	Date	Sender

Bill Log   _____ Month

✓	Date Paid	Bill Name	Amount	Due Date	Confirmation

Mail Tracker

Date	Sender	Date	Sender

Bill Log _____ Month

✓	Date Paid	Bill Name	Amount	Due Date	Confirmation

Mail Tracker

Date	Sender	Date	Sender

Bill Log _____ Month

✓	Date Paid	Bill Name	Amount	Due Date	Confirmation

Mail Tracker

Date	Sender	Date	Sender

Bill Log
_____ Month

✓	Date Paid	Bill Name	Amount	Due Date	Confirmation

Mail Tracker

Date	Sender	Date	Sender

Bill Log _____ Month

✓	Date Paid	Bill Name	Amount	Due Date	Confirmation

Mail Tracker

Date	Sender	Date	Sender

Bill Log _____ Month

✓	Date Paid	Bill Name	Amount	Due Date	Confirmation

Mail Tracker

Date	Sender	Date	Sender

Bill Log _____ Month

✓	Date Paid	Bill Name	Amount	Due Date	Confirmation

Mail Tracker

Date	Sender	Date	Sender

Bill Log _____ Month

✓	Date Paid	Bill Name	Amount	Due Date	Confirmation

Mail Tracker

Date	Sender	Date	Sender

Bill Log

_____ Month

✓	Date Paid	Bill Name	Amount	Due Date	Confirmation

Mail Tracker

Date	Sender	Date	Sender

Bill Log _____ Month

✓	Date Paid	Bill Name	Amount	Due Date	Confirmation

Mail Tracker

Date	Sender	Date	Sender

Bill Log _____ Month

✓	Date Paid	Bill Name	Amount	Due Date	Confirmation

Mail Tracker

Date	Sender	Date	Sender

Bill Log

_____ Month

✓	Date Paid	Bill Name	Amount	Due Date	Confirmation

Mail Tracker

Date	Sender	Date	Sender

Bill Log _____ Month

✓	Date Paid	Bill Name	Amount	Due Date	Confirmation

Mail Tracker

Date	Sender	Date	Sender

Bill Log _____ Month

✓	Date Paid	Bill Name	Amount	Due Date	Confirmation

Mail Tracker

Date	Sender	Date	Sender

Bill Log _____ Month

✓	Date Paid	Bill Name	Amount	Due Date	Confirmation

Mail Tracker

Date	Sender	Date	Sender

Bill Log _____ Month

✓	Date Paid	Bill Name	Amount	Due Date	Confirmation

Mail Tracker

Date	Sender	Date	Sender

Bill Log

_____ Month

✓	Date Paid	Bill Name	Amount	Due Date	Confirmation

Mail Tracker

Date	Sender	Date	Sender

Bill Log _____ Month

✓	Date Paid	Bill Name	Amount	Due Date	Confirmation

Mail Tracker

Date	Sender	Date	Sender

Bill Log

_____ Month

✓	Date Paid	Bill Name	Amount	Due Date	Confirmation

Mail Tracker

Date	Sender	Date	Sender

Bill Log _____ Month

✓	Date Paid	Bill Name	Amount	Due Date	Confirmation

Mail Tracker

Date	Sender	Date	Sender

Bill Log

_____ Month

✓	Date Paid	Bill Name	Amount	Due Date	Confirmation

Mail Tracker

Date	Sender

Date	Sender

Bill Log

_____ Month

✓	Date Paid	Bill Name	Amount	Due Date	Confirmation

Mail Tracker

Date	Sender	Date	Sender

Bill Log

_____ Month

✓	Date Paid	Bill Name	Amount	Due Date	Confirmation

Mail Tracker

Date	Sender	Date	Sender

Bill Log _____ Month

✓	Date Paid	Bill Name	Amount	Due Date	Confirmation

Mail Tracker

Date	Sender

Date	Sender

Bill Log   _____ Month

✓	Date Paid	Bill Name	Amount	Due Date	Confirmation

Mail Tracker

Date	Sender	Date	Sender

Bill Log   _____ Month

✓	Date Paid	Bill Name	Amount	Due Date	Confirmation

Mail Tracker

Date	Sender	Date	Sender

Bill Log   _____ Month

✓	Date Paid	Bill Name	Amount	Due Date	Confirmation

Mail Tracker

Date	Sender	Date	Sender

Bill Log
_____ Month

✓	Date Paid	Bill Name	Amount	Due Date	Confirmation

Mail Tracker

Date	Sender

Date	Sender

Bill Log
_____ Month

✓	Date Paid	Bill Name	Amount	Due Date	Confirmation

Mail Tracker

Date	Sender	Date	Sender

Bill Log _____ Month

✓	Date Paid	Bill Name	Amount	Due Date	Confirmation

Mail Tracker

Date	Sender

Date	Sender

Bill Log _____ Month

✓	Date Paid	Bill Name	Amount	Due Date	Confirmation

Mail Tracker

Date	Sender	Date	Sender

Bill Log _____ Month

✓	Date Paid	Bill Name	Amount	Due Date	Confirmation

Mail Tracker

Date	Sender	Date	Sender

Bill Log _____ Month

✓	Date Paid	Bill Name	Amount	Due Date	Confirmation

Mail Tracker

Date	Sender	Date	Sender

Bill Log _____ Month

✓	Date Paid	Bill Name	Amount	Due Date	Confirmation

Mail Tracker

Date	Sender	Date	Sender

Bill Log _____ Month

✓	Date Paid	Bill Name	Amount	Due Date	Confirmation

Mail Tracker

Date	Sender	Date	Sender

Bill Log _____ Month

✓	Date Paid	Bill Name	Amount	Due Date	Confirmation

Mail Tracker

Date	Sender	Date	Sender

Bill Log _____ Month

✓	Date Paid	Bill Name	Amount	Due Date	Confirmation

Mail Tracker

Date	Sender	Date	Sender

Bill Log _____ Month

✓	Date Paid	Bill Name	Amount	Due Date	Confirmation

Mail Tracker

Date	Sender	Date	Sender

Bill Log _____ Month

✓	Date Paid	Bill Name	Amount	Due Date	Confirmation

Mail Tracker

Date	Sender	Date	Sender

Bill Log _____ Month

✓	Date Paid	Bill Name	Amount	Due Date	Confirmation

Mail Tracker

Date	Sender	Date	Sender

Bill Log

_____ Month

✓	Date Paid	Bill Name	Amount	Due Date	Confirmation

Mail Tracker

Date	Sender	Date	Sender

Bill Log _____ Month

✓	Date Paid	Bill Name	Amount	Due Date	Confirmation

Mail Tracker

Date	Sender	Date	Sender

Bill Log _____ Month

✓	Date Paid	Bill Name	Amount	Due Date	Confirmation

Mail Tracker

Date	Sender	Date	Sender

Bill Log _____ Month

✓	Date Paid	Bill Name	Amount	Due Date	Confirmation

Mail Tracker

Date	Sender	Date	Sender

Bill Log
_____ Month

✓	Date Paid	Bill Name	Amount	Due Date	Confirmation

Mail Tracker

Date	Sender	Date	Sender

Bill Log

_____ Month

✓	Date Paid	Bill Name	Amount	Due Date	Confirmation

Mail Tracker

Date	Sender	Date	Sender

Bill Log _____ Month

✓	Date Paid	Bill Name	Amount	Due Date	Confirmation

Mail Tracker

Date	Sender	Date	Sender

Bill Log _____ Month

✓	Date Paid	Bill Name	Amount	Due Date	Confirmation

Mail Tracker

Date	Sender	Date	Sender

Bill Log _____ Month

✓	Date Paid	Bill Name	Amount	Due Date	Confirmation

Mail Tracker

Date	Sender	Date	Sender

Bill Log

_____ Month

✓	Date Paid	Bill Name	Amount	Due Date	Confirmation

Mail Tracker

Date	Sender

Date	Sender

Bill Log _____ Month

✓	Date Paid	Bill Name	Amount	Due Date	Confirmation

Mail Tracker

Date	Sender	Date	Sender

Bill Log _____ Month

✓	Date Paid	Bill Name	Amount	Due Date	Confirmation

Mail Tracker

Date	Sender	Date	Sender

Bill Log

_____ Month

✓	Date Paid	Bill Name	Amount	Due Date	Confirmation

Mail Tracker

Date	Sender	Date	Sender

Bill Log

_____ Month

✓	Date Paid	Bill Name	Amount	Due Date	Confirmation

Mail Tracker

Date	Sender	Date	Sender

Bill Log _____ Month

✓	Date Paid	Bill Name	Amount	Due Date	Confirmation

Mail Tracker

Date	Sender	Date	Sender

Bill Log

_____ Month

✓	Date Paid	Bill Name	Amount	Due Date	Confirmation

Mail Tracker

Date	Sender	Date	Sender

Bill Log _____ Month

✓	Date Paid	Bill Name	Amount	Due Date	Confirmation

Mail Tracker

Date	Sender	Date	Sender

Bill Log _____ Month

✓	Date Paid	Bill Name	Amount	Due Date	Confirmation

Mail Tracker

Date	Sender	Date	Sender

Bill Log

_____ Month

✓	Date Paid	Bill Name	Amount	Due Date	Confirmation

Mail Tracker

Date	Sender	Date	Sender

Bill Log
_____ Month

✓	Date Paid	Bill Name	Amount	Due Date	Confirmation

Mail Tracker

Date	Sender	Date	Sender

Bill Log _____ Month

✓	Date Paid	Bill Name	Amount	Due Date	Confirmation

Mail Tracker

Date	Sender	Date	Sender

Bill Log _____ Month

✓	Date Paid	Bill Name	Amount	Due Date	Confirmation

Mail Tracker

Date	Sender	Date	Sender

Bill Log _____ Month

✓	Date Paid	Bill Name	Amount	Due Date	Confirmation

Mail Tracker

Date	Sender	Date	Sender

Bill Log _____ Month

✓	Date Paid	Bill Name	Amount	Due Date	Confirmation

Mail Tracker

Date	Sender

Date	Sender

Bill Log _____ Month

✓	Date Paid	Bill Name	Amount	Due Date	Confirmation

Mail Tracker

Date	Sender	Date	Sender

Bill Log _____ Month

✓	Date Paid	Bill Name	Amount	Due Date	Confirmation

Mail Tracker

Date	Sender	Date	Sender

Bill Log _____ Month

✓	Date Paid	Bill Name	Amount	Due Date	Confirmation

Mail Tracker

Date	Sender	Date	Sender

Bill Log _____ Month

✓	Date Paid	Bill Name	Amount	Due Date	Confirmation

Mail Tracker

Date	Sender	Date	Sender

Bill Log
_____ Month

✓	Date Paid	Bill Name	Amount	Due Date	Confirmation

Mail Tracker

Date	Sender	Date	Sender

Bill Log _____ Month

✓	Date Paid	Bill Name	Amount	Due Date	Confirmation

Mail Tracker

Date	Sender	Date	Sender

Bill Log
_____ Month

✓	Date Paid	Bill Name	Amount	Due Date	Confirmation

Mail Tracker

Date	Sender	Date	Sender

Bill Log _____ Month

✓	Date Paid	Bill Name	Amount	Due Date	Confirmation

Mail Tracker

Date	Sender	Date	Sender

Bill Log

_____ Month

✓	Date Paid	Bill Name	Amount	Due Date	Confirmation

Mail Tracker

Date	Sender	Date	Sender

Bill Log _____ Month

✓	Date Paid	Bill Name	Amount	Due Date	Confirmation

Mail Tracker

Date	Sender	Date	Sender

Bill Log _____ Month

✓	Date Paid	Bill Name	Amount	Due Date	Confirmation

Mail Tracker

Date	Sender	Date	Sender

Bill Log _____ Month

✓	Date Paid	Bill Name	Amount	Due Date	Confirmation

Mail Tracker

Date	Sender	Date	Sender

Bill Log

_____ Month

✓	Date Paid	Bill Name	Amount	Due Date	Confirmation

Mail Tracker

Date	Sender	Date	Sender

Bill Log

_____ Month

✓	Date Paid	Bill Name	Amount	Due Date	Confirmation

Mail Tracker

Date	Sender	Date	Sender

Bill Log _____ Month

✓	Date Paid	Bill Name	Amount	Due Date	Confirmation

Mail Tracker

Date	Sender

Date	Sender

Bill Log

_____ Month

✓	Date Paid	Bill Name	Amount	Due Date	Confirmation

Mail Tracker

Date	Sender

Date	Sender

Bill Log _____ Month

✓	Date Paid	Bill Name	Amount	Due Date	Confirmation

Mail Tracker

Date	Sender	Date	Sender

Bill Log _____ Month

✓	Date Paid	Bill Name	Amount	Due Date	Confirmation

Mail Tracker

Date	Sender	Date	Sender

Bill Log
_____ Month

✓	Date Paid	Bill Name	Amount	Due Date	Confirmation

Mail Tracker

Date	Sender

Date	Sender

Bill Log _____ Month

✓	Date Paid	Bill Name	Amount	Due Date	Confirmation

Mail Tracker

Date	Sender

Date	Sender

Bill Log

_____ Month

✓	Date Paid	Bill Name	Amount	Due Date	Confirmation

Mail Tracker

Date	Sender	Date	Sender

Bill Log _____ Month

✓	Date Paid	Bill Name	Amount	Due Date	Confirmation

Mail Tracker

Date	Sender	Date	Sender

Bill Log

_____ Month

✓	Date Paid	Bill Name	Amount	Due Date	Confirmation

Mail Tracker

Date	Sender

Date	Sender

Bill Log _____ Month

✓	Date Paid	Bill Name	Amount	Due Date	Confirmation

Mail Tracker

Date	Sender	Date	Sender

Bill Log _____ Month

✓	Date Paid	Bill Name	Amount	Due Date	Confirmation

Mail Tracker

Date	Sender	Date	Sender

Bill Log _____ Month

✓	Date Paid	Bill Name	Amount	Due Date	Confirmation

Mail Tracker

Date	Sender	Date	Sender

Bill Log _____ Month

✓	Date Paid	Bill Name	Amount	Due Date	Confirmation

Mail Tracker

Date	Sender	Date	Sender

Bill Log
_____ Month

✓	Date Paid	Bill Name	Amount	Due Date	Confirmation

Mail Tracker

Date	Sender	Date	Sender

Bill Log _____ Month

✓	Date Paid	Bill Name	Amount	Due Date	Confirmation

Mail Tracker

Date	Sender	Date	Sender

Bill Log _____ Month

✓	Date Paid	Bill Name	Amount	Due Date	Confirmation

Mail Tracker

Date	Sender	Date	Sender

Bill Log

_____ Month

✓	Date Paid	Bill Name	Amount	Due Date	Confirmation

Mail Tracker

Date	Sender	Date	Sender

Bill Log _____ Month

✓	Date Paid	Bill Name	Amount	Due Date	Confirmation

Mail Tracker

Date	Sender	Date	Sender

Bill Log _____ Month

✓	Date Paid	Bill Name	Amount	Due Date	Confirmation

Mail Tracker

Date	Sender	Date	Sender

Bill Log _____ Month

✓	Date Paid	Bill Name	Amount	Due Date	Confirmation

Mail Tracker

Date	Sender	Date	Sender

Bill Log _____ Month

✓	Date Paid	Bill Name	Amount	Due Date	Confirmation

Mail Tracker

Date	Sender	Date	Sender

Bill Log _____ Month

✓	Date Paid	Bill Name	Amount	Due Date	Confirmation

Mail Tracker

Date	Sender	Date	Sender

Bill Log _____ Month

✓	Date Paid	Bill Name	Amount	Due Date	Confirmation

Mail Tracker

Date	Sender	Date	Sender

Bill Log _____ Month

✓	Date Paid	Bill Name	Amount	Due Date	Confirmation

Mail Tracker

Date	Sender	Date	Sender

CPSIA information can be obtained
at www.ICGtesting.com
Printed in the USA
LVHW060303180123
737399LV00010B/531